What Makes My Dad Special?

Written by C. Selbherr

Illustrated by Nugraha

Copyright © 2018 by Harlescott Books

All rights reserved. This book or any portion thereof may not be reproduced or used in any manner whatsoever without the express written permission of the author except for the use of brief quotations in a book review.

ISBN-13: 978-3-947677-09-2 (Harlescott Books)

As far as parents go, I feel like I hit the jackpot. My parents were and still are thoughtful, kind, loving and supportive.

But not everyone has the luck that I have had. Sometimes fathers or mothers just aren't around. Sometimes through no fault of their own and sometimes it's just not possible for that parent to be a part of a child's life.

Sometimes the single parent meets and falls in love with a new partner. If you are lucky, your new partner will love and cherish your child as much as he/she does you. The bond between a step parent and a child can be an amazing thing. But what if your child doesn't know that their mom or dad isn't their biological parent? Have you found yourself wondering how and when to tell your child? Many parents find themselves in this situation. Do I tell my child early? Or in their teens? Or as an adult?

If you have decided to tell your child early, then I hope that this picture book will help you. It is full of wonderful illustrations that will encourage you to discuss this theme with your son or daughter. It is an ideal first step in explaining the love a step parent can feel for their child.

Happy reading!
Charlotte

One day Mom and Kate were playing in the garden.

Kate – with many questions – said, "Mom, I beg your pardon…

…but what makes my dad special?"
She asked with a stare.

"Sit down and I will tell you."
Mom pulled out a chair.

Mom took a deep breath and sat next to Kate.

"I'll tell you the story of why your dad is so great!"

"He used to change your diaper when you were so small…

...he followed you around the house when you began to crawl."

"He fed you in your high chair and always wiped your nose…

…kept your hands nice and clean, he even washed your toes."

"He held your hand tightly when you began to walk…

...listened to your mumbling, when you started to talk."

"He watched you at nursery school on your very first day…

...you were nervous and quite shy.
You asked him, "Please? Do stay!"

"He watched you ride a bike for the very first time…

...waited below to catch you when you wanted to climb."

"He taught you how to cook and you both made dinner…

…he never let you feel sad, you were always his winner."

"He cleaned you up, and brushed you off whenever you fell down…

...dried your tears and cheered you up,
took away your frown."

"He sat with other parents and watched you sing at school…

...he made sure you didn't swallow too much water at the pool."

"He showed you how to tie your laces when you didn't know…

...he took you sledding on the hills outside in the snow."

Mom said: "I picked a special dad, just for me and you.
I met him when you were a baby, our love blossomed and grew."

"You sat next to us at church when we got married.
You wore a beautiful dress with the flowers that you carried."

"I hope you understand why your dad's a special man...

...he loves you to the moon and back, he's your biggest fan."

Dad said:

"I'm so proud that you call me dad, dear little Kate.

Our family is wonderful and amazingly great.

I am very lucky and so happy that we,

Are a fabulous family. You, your mom and me."

Lightning Source UK Ltd.
Milton Keynes UK
UKRC012021241019
352260UK00001B/1